The Giant Whale Returns

Aariz Ansari

GULF BOOK SERVICES

The contents of this work, including, but not limited to, the accuracy of events, people, and places depicted; opinions expressed; permission to use previously published materials included; and any advice given, or actions advocated are solely the responsibility of the author, who assumes all liabilities for the said work and indemnifies the publisher against any claims stemming from publication of the work.

All Rights Reserved
© Aariz Ansari

Published by Gulf Book Services Ltd
20 - 22 Wenlock Road, London,
NI 7GU, UK
Email: info@gulfbooks.co.uk
Office No: G23, Sharjah Publishing City Free Zone
Sharjah – UAE

First Published by Gulf Book Services Ltd

No part of this book may be reproduced or transmitted, downloaded, distributed, reverse engineered, or stored in or introduced into any information storage and retrieval system, in any form or by any means, including photocopying and recording, whether electronic or mechanical, now known or hereinafter invented without permission in writing from the publisher.

ISBN: 978-1-917529-27-3
Year: Sept 2025

Book Cover:
Compiled & Illustration : Rohan Menon & Madhavi. S

The Giant Whale Returns

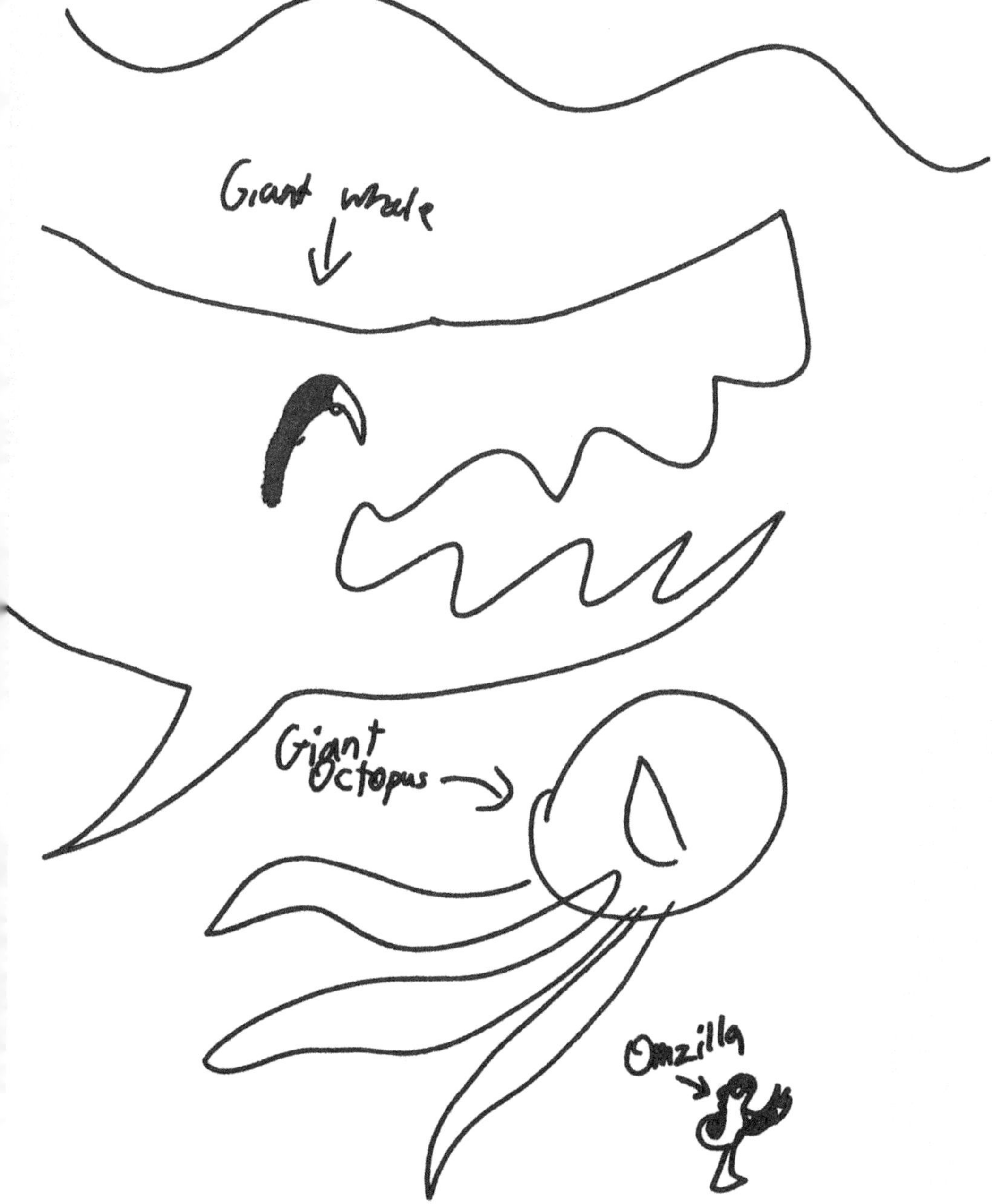

Giant whale ↓

Giant Octopus →

Omzilla →

1

Mothra — Rodan — king Ghidorah

Giant shark

Godzilla — Angirus

Giant crocodile

2

Chapter 1

I found you!

(Enjoy)

Shoutout to: Om, Ahmed Metwally, Donovan and Faris JO 3 OJAS (and Mark S)

Chapter 2
Creating an army

Panel 2: "Heh"

Panel 3: "Godzilla won't see what's about to hit him"

Panel 4: "HAHAHA" "that is a normal whale" "HAHAHA" "HAHAHA"

Chapter 3

They are on our tails!

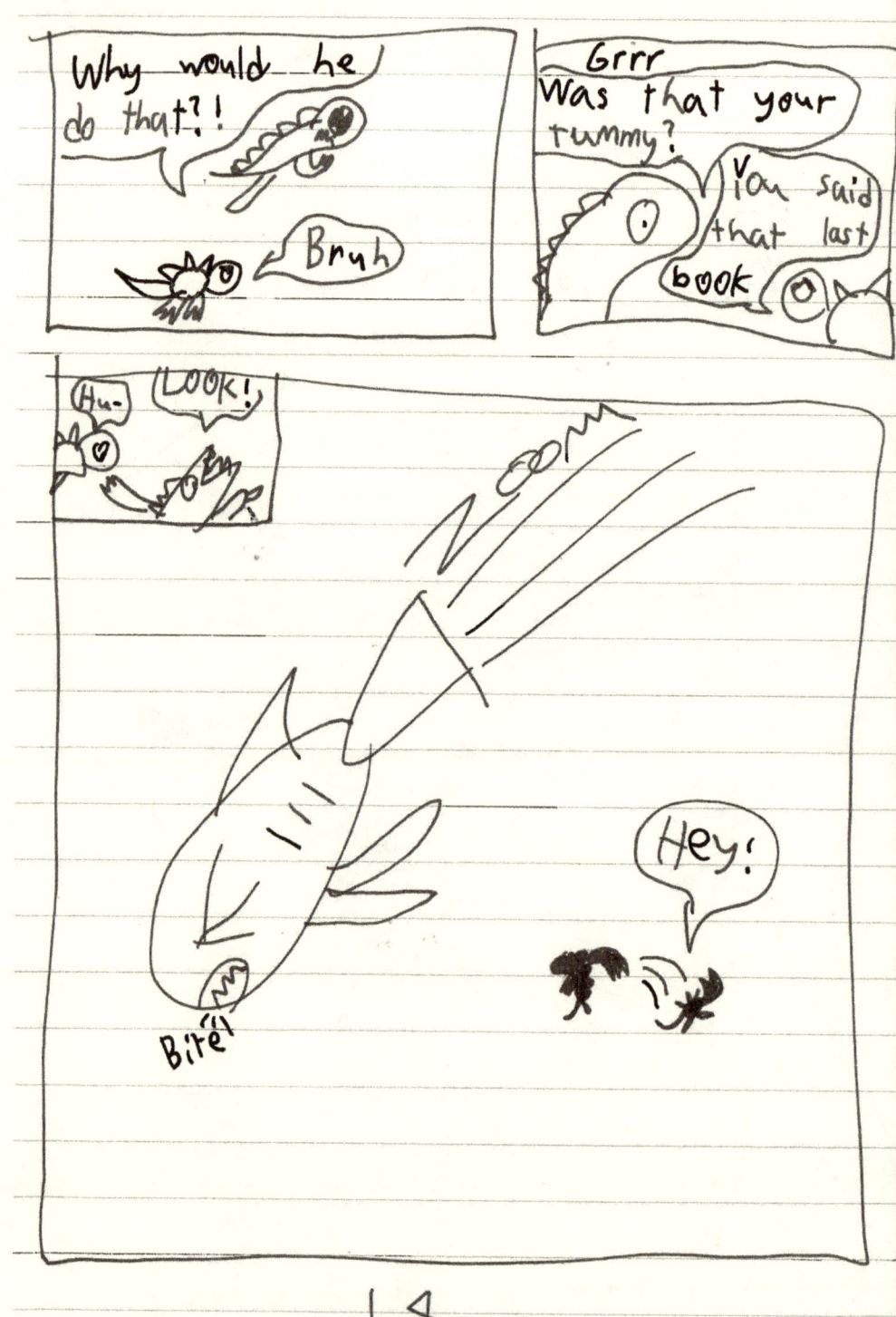

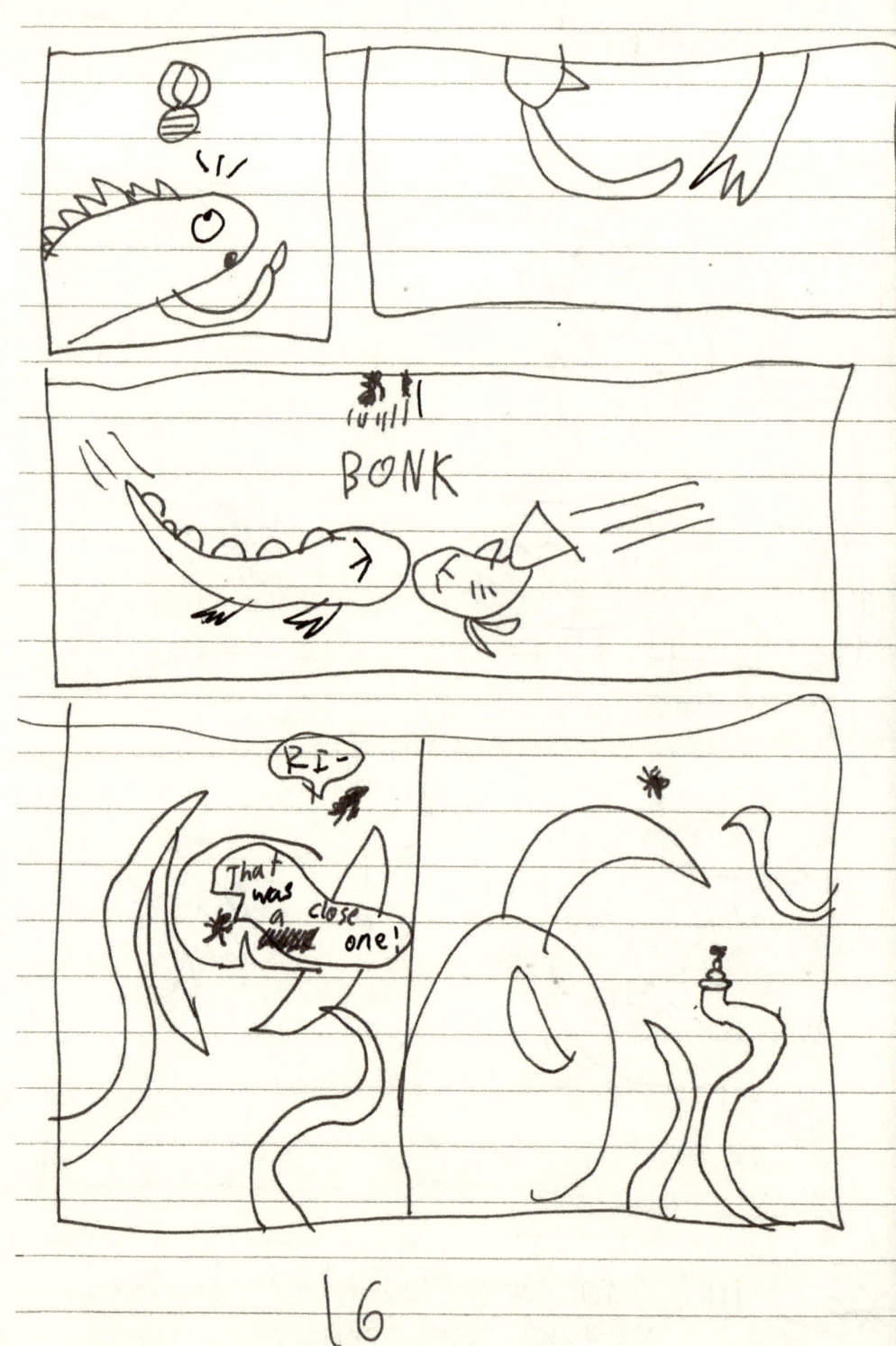

Chapter 4

I can't swim!

Chapter 5

Rodan vs lizilla's

SHOUTOUT FOR: OM!!! 10/10

Chapter 6
INCOMING!!!

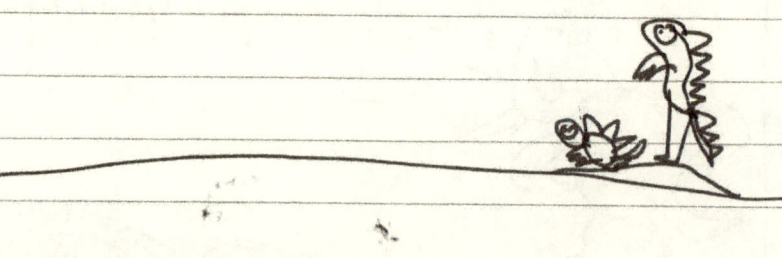

"Will we ever slow down?"

"Uhhh..." "hopefully"

meanwhile...
"It's good to be back!"

"Where are the others?" "Idk"

29

30

Shoutout to: OM yaaaY!

Chapter 7
Cartoon logic

Chapter 8

A Not-so happy reunion

Chapter 8.5

The shortest chapter ever writen

Chapter 9

The battle of the clones (sort of)

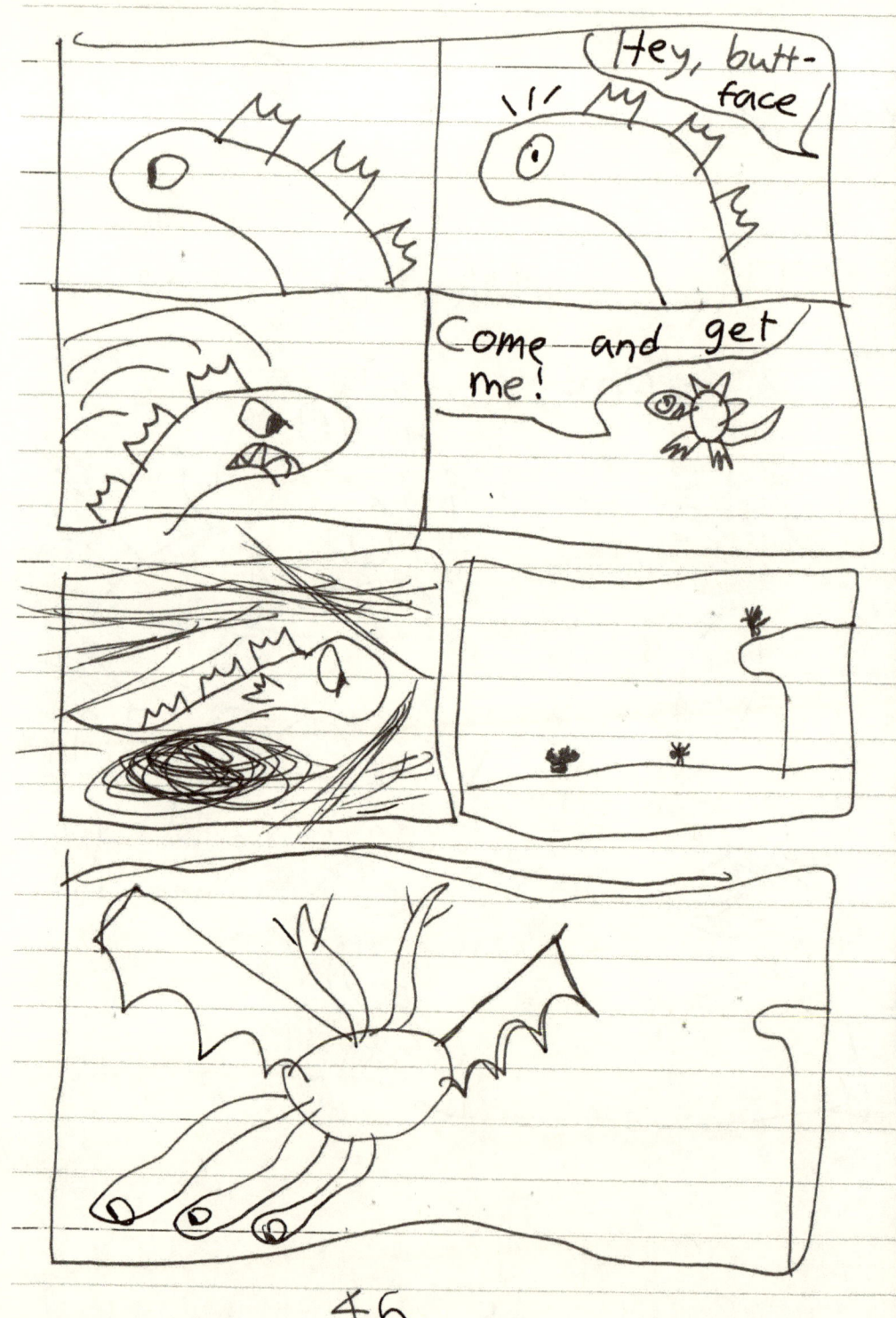

Chapter 10
I think we know what's happening

Chapter 11

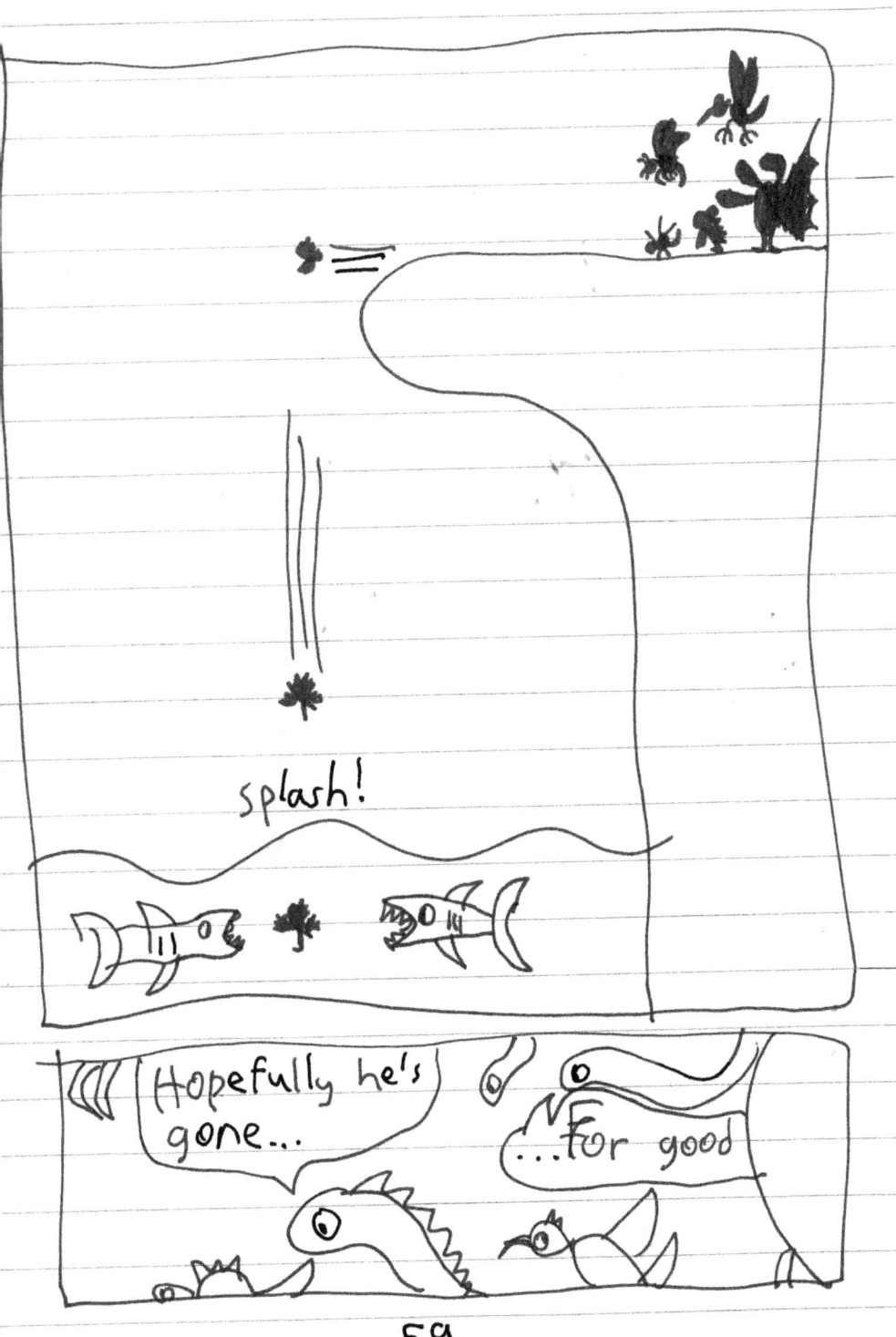

Chapter 12

Why we are here

Yay! You guys saved us!
thanks
Bruh
Well we didn't actually come to sav-
WHAT?

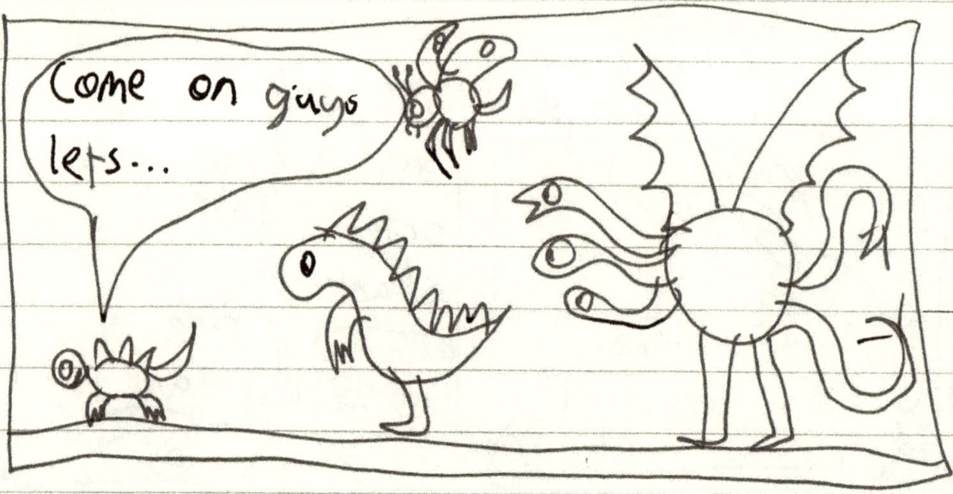
Come on guys lets...

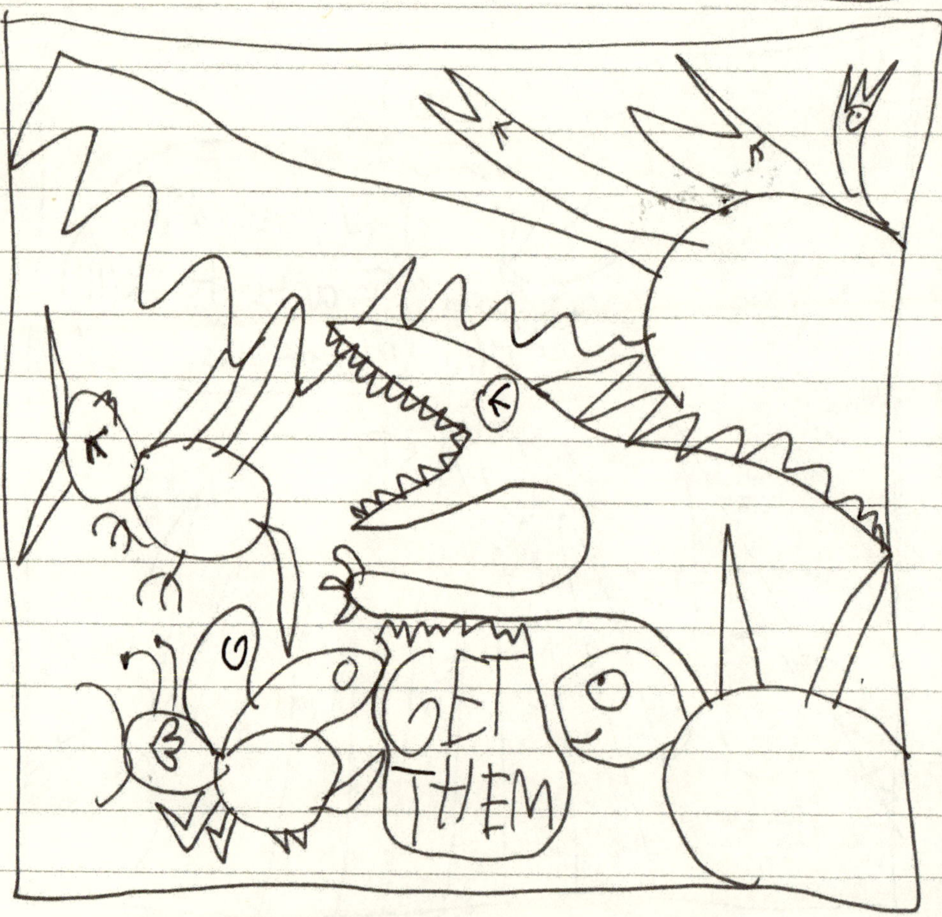
GET THEM

Chapter 13

I see somthing approching the ~~[scribble]~~ land

Chapter 14
plan 1: digging

Chapter 15

plan 2: flying

75

Chapter by Om-Om wrote this BTW

Chapter 16
"Peace" day

Ojas idia ~~Ojas Idea~~

chapter 17
The big fight (plus Ojas)
          ↙
the Ojas Godwani
warzone

Pew!

Pew!

Pew!

85

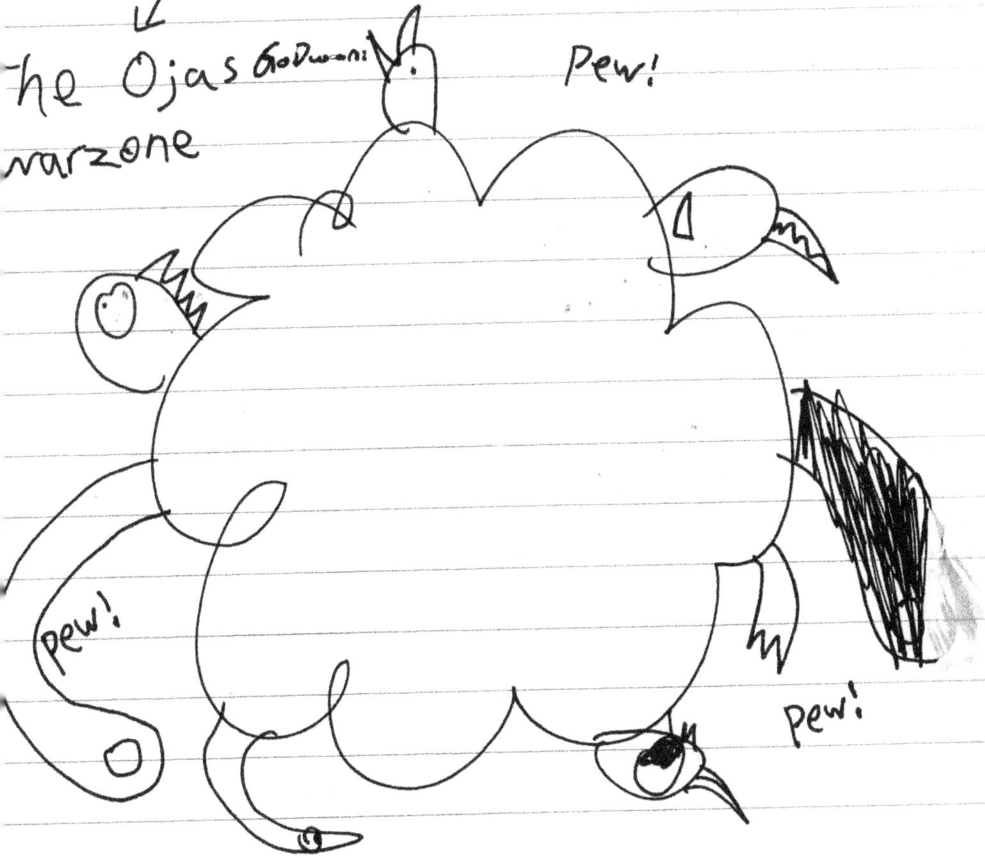

Chapter 18
Back to the Croc

You know what, lets fight the giant crocodile
But we retreated on page 67
And we tried 2 plans but they failed
IDC!!
WE ARE SHOWING HIM WHAT WE ARE MADE OF!!
Okay
LETS DO THIS!

Chapter 19
the kracken (this is also the giant octopus)

This is Om's other idea

Chapter 20

a vision

Chapter 21

Chomp! Chomp! Chomp!

Chapter 22
A favor

This might be a short chapter

How did you do it?
Well I'll tell you... With...
Flip o ra-
No, we don't include Flip o ramas in these seri
Sorry reader
We call it
Flash back!

Chapter 22.5

Flashback!

Chapter 23

My head is gone!

This chapter might be gory. If you like violence, you can read this chapter. If you don't like violence, skip the chapter.

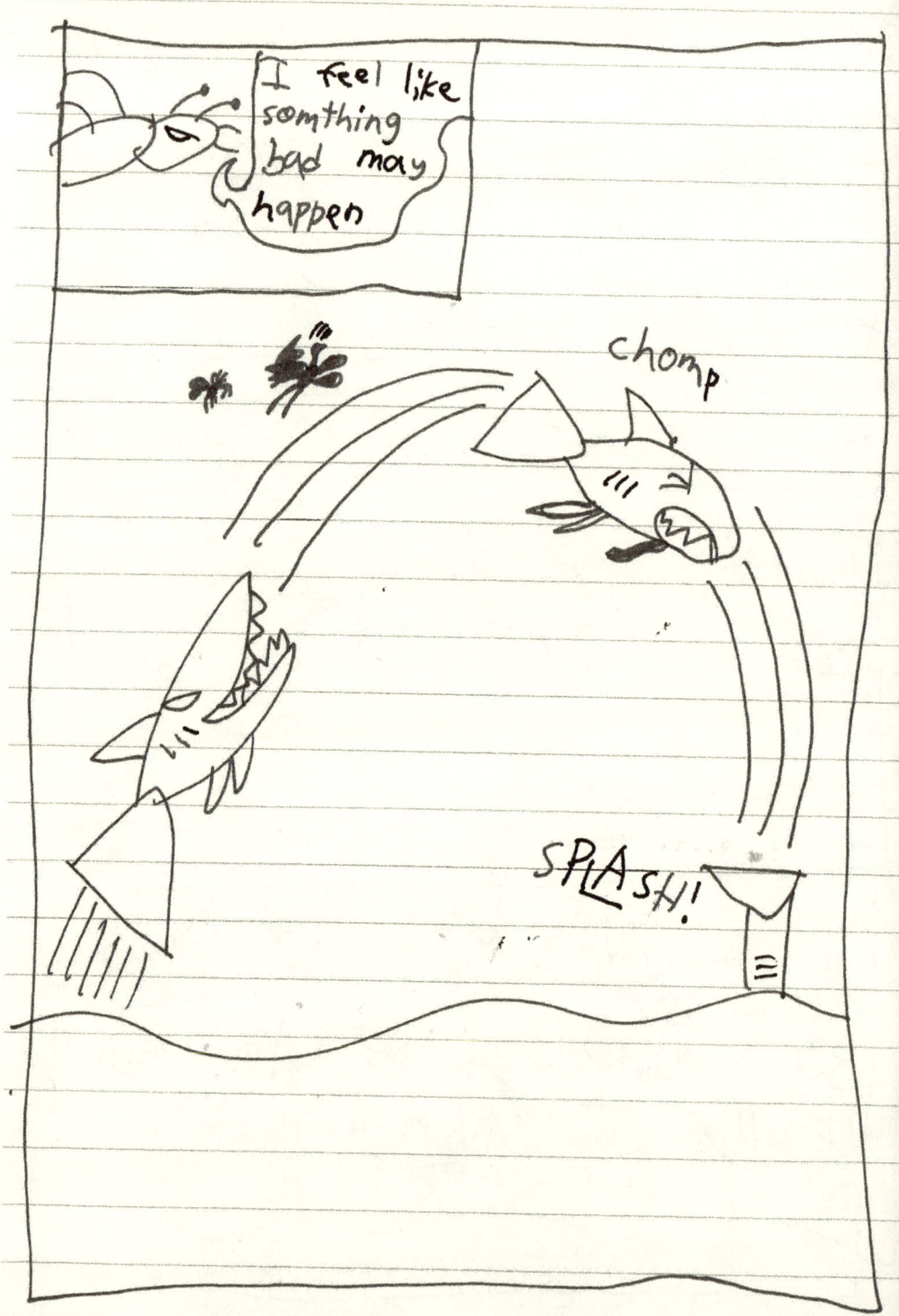

HOLY SHEESH TAWOOK! NI'S HEAD CAME OF
DON'T SLIP!
PHEW I'm SAFE!
We need to find Rodan first
Found'em
YEAH, but where?

Chapter 24

Guys! Look what happend!

"HUMANZILLA!"

"This is Humanzilla, he will help you"

"Thanks!"

"screech!"

"LETS DO THIS!"

monday/28th/October 2024

But before we continue on... I want to say: YAAAAY!

I got the cake.

HAPPY BIRTHDAY OMG

Just say happy Birthday

who is OM?

I have revived because of this celebration! so crazy!

128

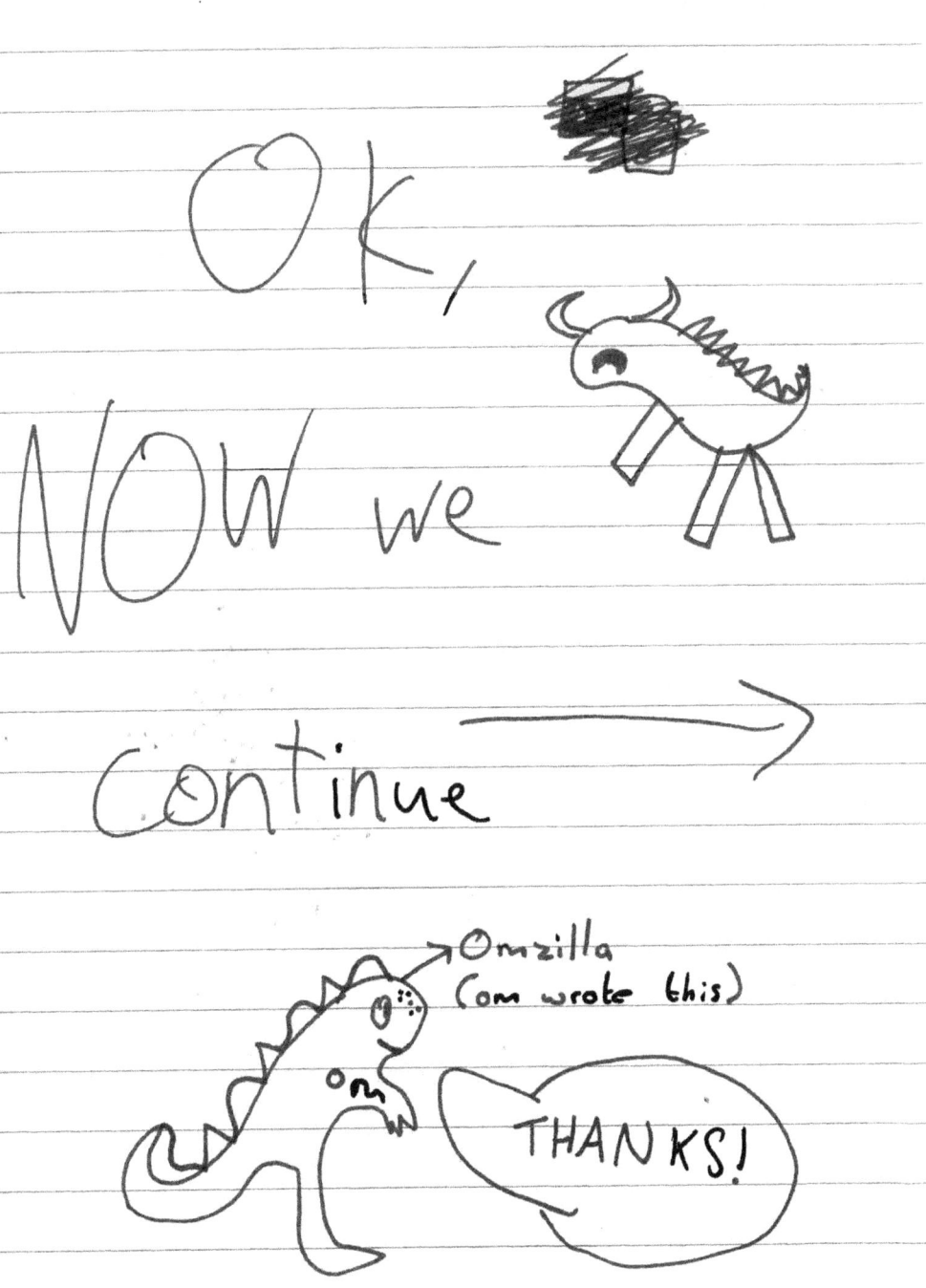

Chapter 25
training

Ok... so before we go to fight, you must train.
I have prepared 100 lizilla's that I ~~kit~~ kidnapped from their homes
What did you say
And go fight!

"Wow... You killed them all!"

"Impressive!"

"Next tak!"

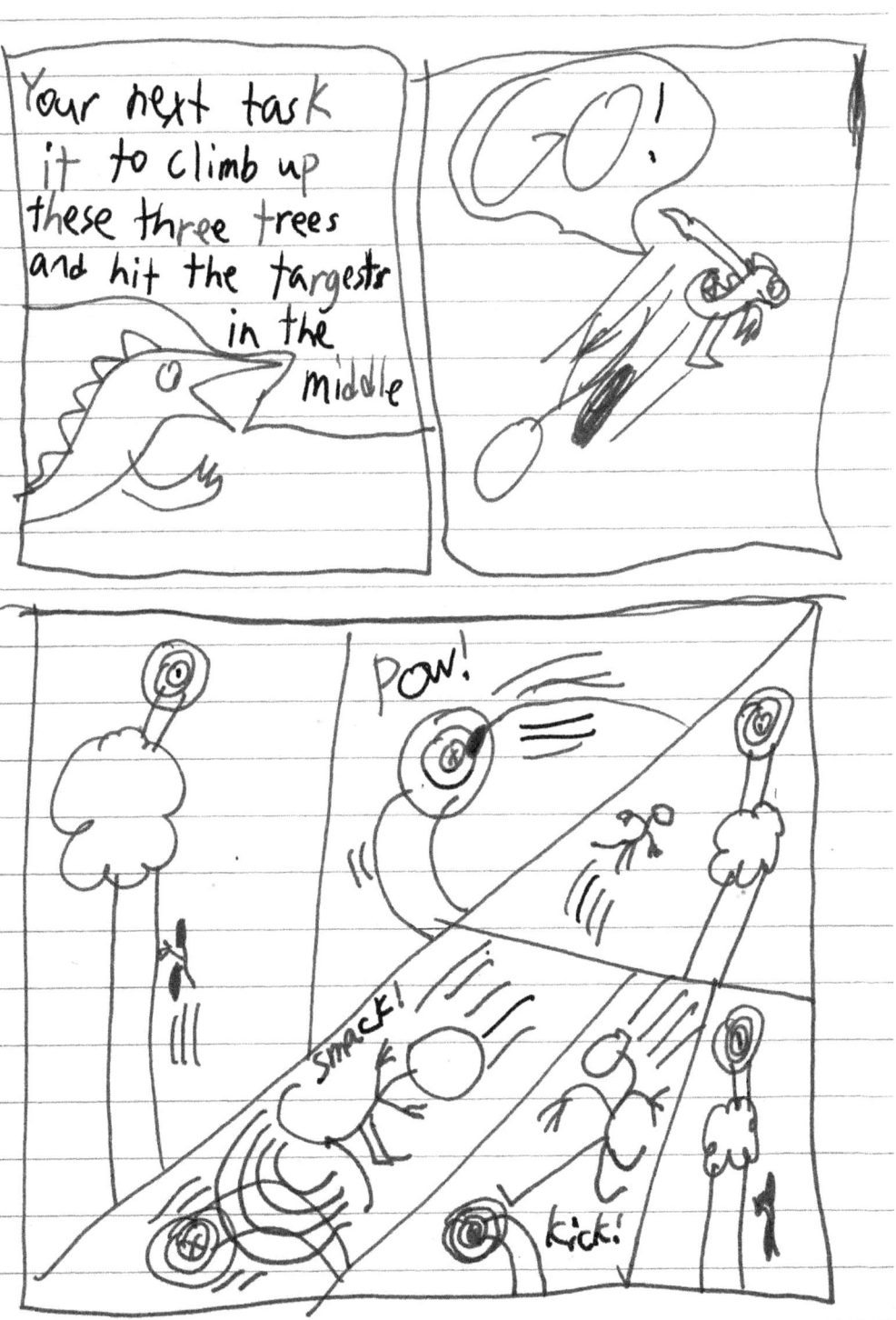

Chapter 26

Mission: Starting

135

then!
Nice!
Whoru
I'm Omzilla!
How many versions of me are there?
ROAR!
Don't hurt them!
Knife

Chapter 27

Into the depths

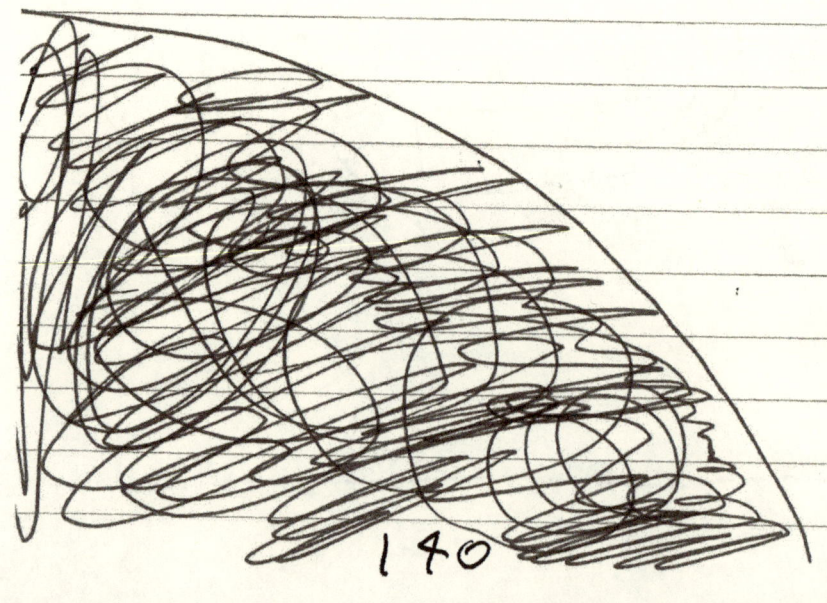

Oh ... Yeah... About that
What do you mean?
Say what now?
We killed them!
So are you a scardey whale?
You messed with the wrong whale buddy!

Chapter 28

The final battle

| Panel 2: "why does he keep doing that?"

Panel 3: "Then... Woah! what's happening~"

Panel 6: "Punch!"

Panel 7: "what's happening?"

147

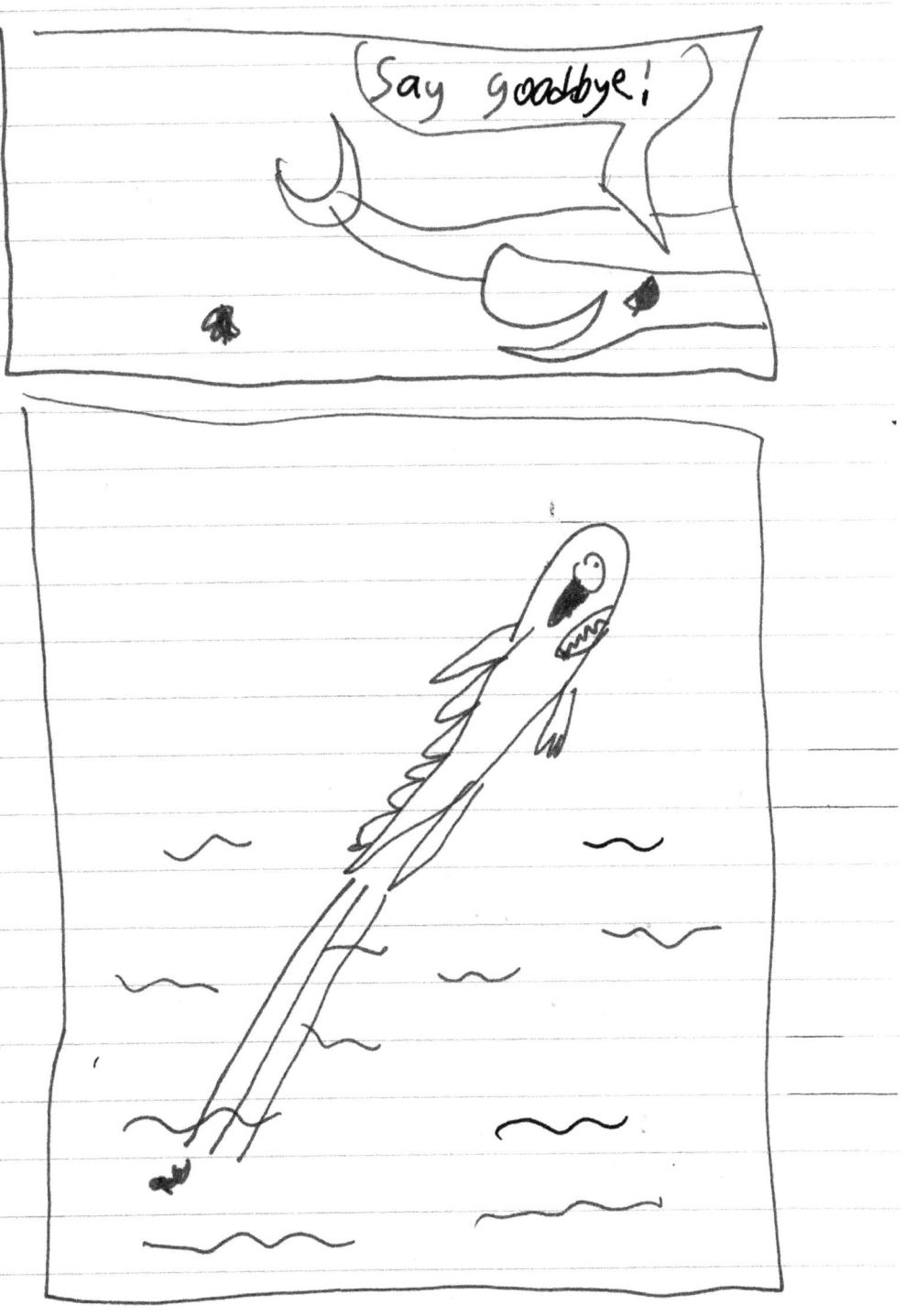

Chapter 28.5
The end of Godzilla?

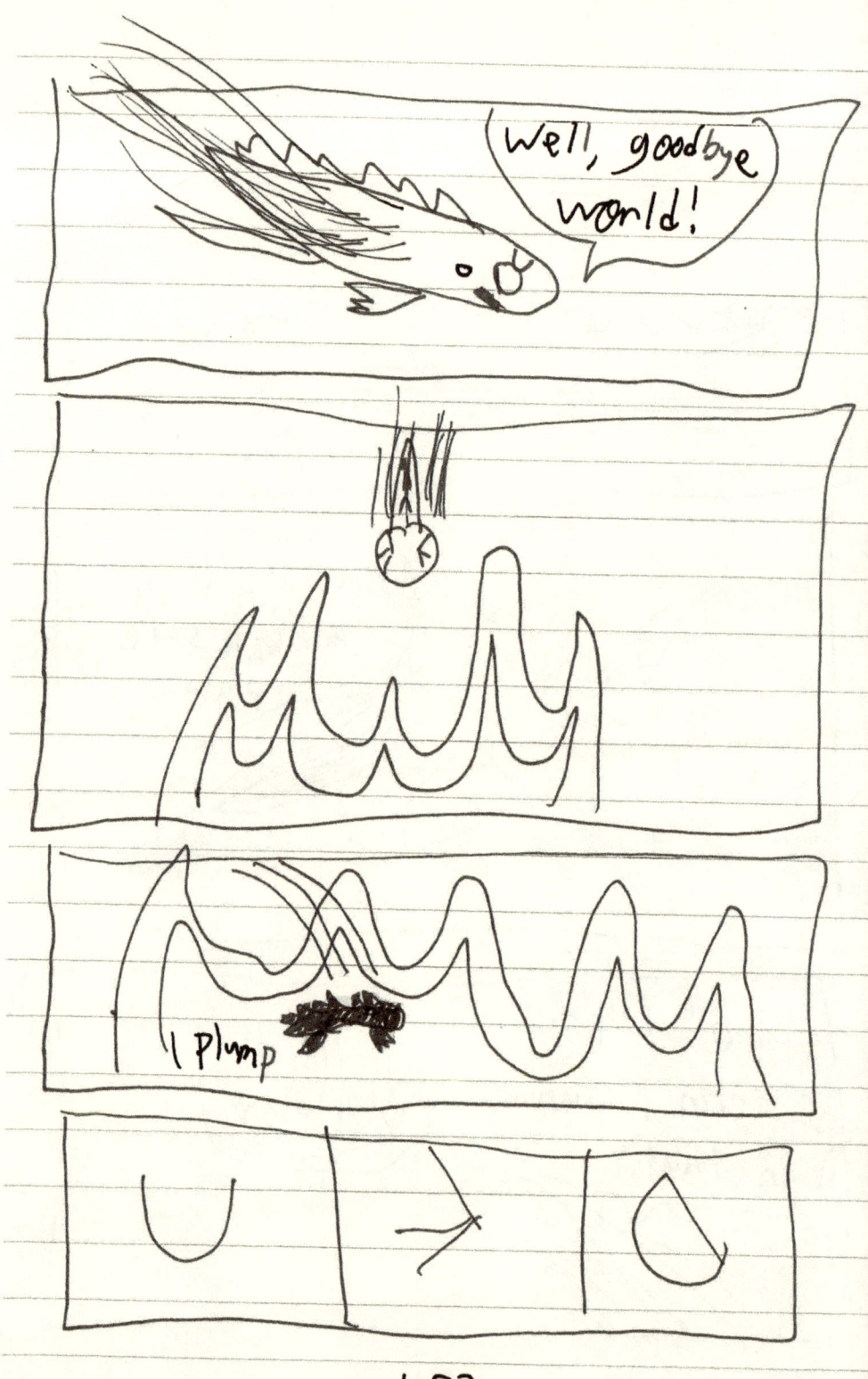

Chapter 29

RETREAT

Chapter 30
(The final chapter)

An introduction to the Book #3

How to draw the characters (step by step)

How to draw: Godzilla minus One (properly)

1. C
2. C
3. ⌒
4. ⊙
5. ⊙
6. ⊙
7. ⊙
8. ⊙
9. ⊙
10. ⊙
11. ⊙

How to draw: The giant whale!

1.
2.
3.
4.
5.
6.
7.
8.
9.
10.
11.
12.

163

How to draw: the giant crocodi[le]

~~For~~ do steps 7-7 from the giant whale and continue with this↓

8.
9.
10.
11.
12.
13.

How to draw: The giant shark!!

1. |
2. ◁
3. ⌀◁
4. ⊚◁
5. ⌀◁ (with fin)
6. ⌀◁ (with fins)
7. ⌀◁ (with fins)
8. ⌀||◁ (with fins)
9. 🦈

How to draw: The "peace" doves

1.
2.
3.
4.
5.
6.
7.
8.
9.
10.
11.

L67

How to draw: The King of the "peace" doves

~~continue from~~ do steps 1-3 from the "peace" doves and continue with this ↓

7.
10.
11.
12.
13.
14.

15.
16.

168

BONUS!

How to draw: The gun for

EXTRA! the "peace" doves!

BONUS — Draw the aim!

1. ∪
2. ◝
3. ◕
4. ▰

5. ▰
6. ▰

169

How to draw: Humanzilla!

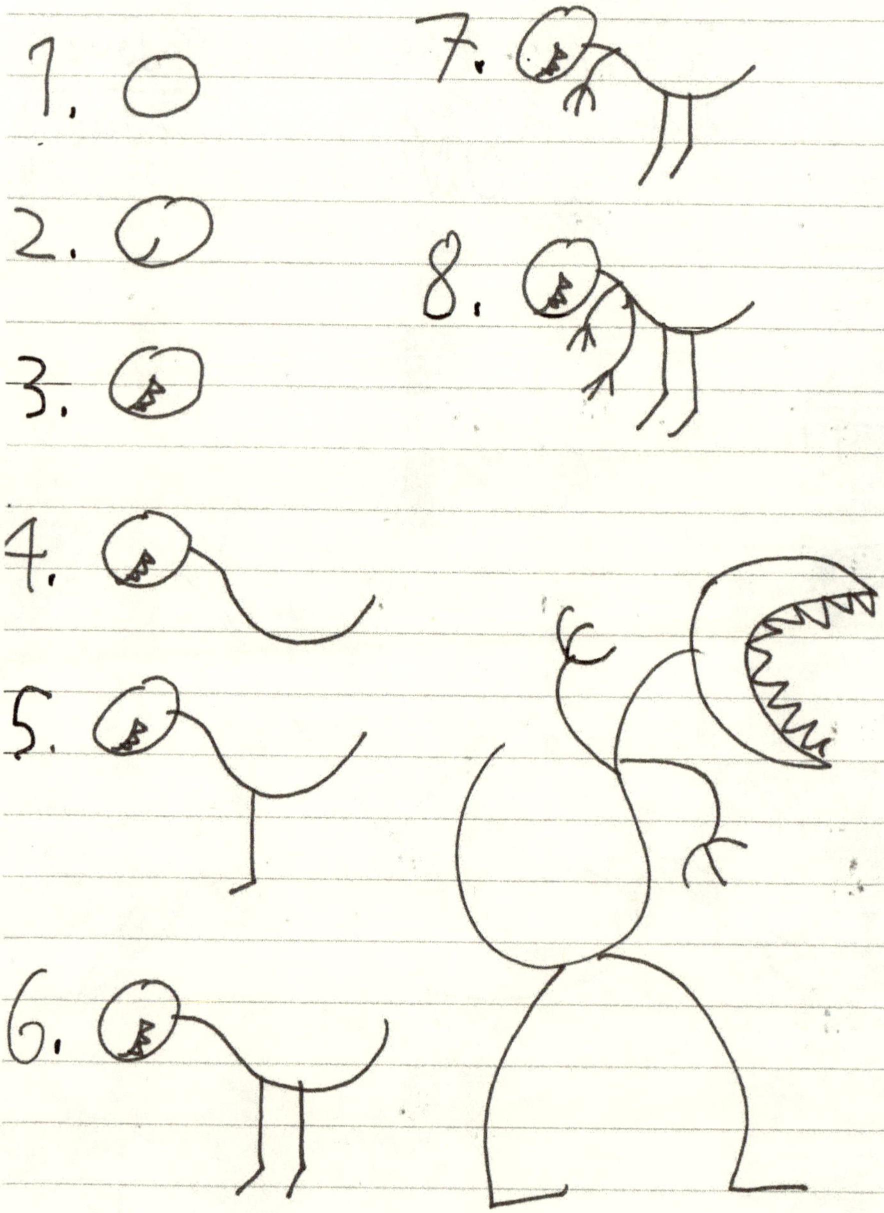

1. O
2. ⊙
3. ⊙
4. ⊙—
5. ⊙—|
6. ⊙—/\
7. ⊙—
8. ⊙—/\

How to draw: Onzilla!

1. C
2. C
3. C
4. C
5. C O
6. C O
7. C O
8.
9.
10.
11.
10.
11.
12.

171

My Parents rating of the book.

AARIZ IS VERY PASSIONATE ABOUT HIS COMIC CREATION. THIS IS HIS SECOND EDITION AFTER "MINUS ONE SITUATION". YOU WILL ENJOY READING THIS COMIC AND YOUR INTEREST WILL BUILD UP FOR FURTHER EDITIONS..

Nayyar Ansari

The story is expertly woven as a part two from his first book; The Minus One Situation. There are complex narratives that explore different stories. Aariz has a colorful and creative imagination in which he builds his world to tell a story. Its his own universe which is both fascinating and impressive. We can see his passion in his story telling - it shines through on every page.

Nasheela Khan

My friends rating of the book

Om's Rating (Omzilla)   *Om drew this*

The book is a 9/10 (I didn't even read the book yet) (Dont tell Aariz)

Ojas Goduani Rating

The book Great I Loved it 10/10

Arsh's Rating (Bobzilla)

I loved it! Definitely one of the best books I have read in a Long, Long time. 10/10

Wait!

Before I say Bye.

I forgot one more character in the "how to draw" tutorials.

How to draw: The Lizilla Combination

do steps 1-7 from the giant whale and continue with this

8.

9.

10.

11.

12.

13.

Now add some parts!

eye	Arm/Leg	Tail	spike
1. ⬭	2. ▓▓▓	1. ∼	1. ╱
2. ⬭	1. ╱	2. ∽	2. ⋀
3. ⬭	2. ⋀	3. 〈teeth〉	

Examples:

182

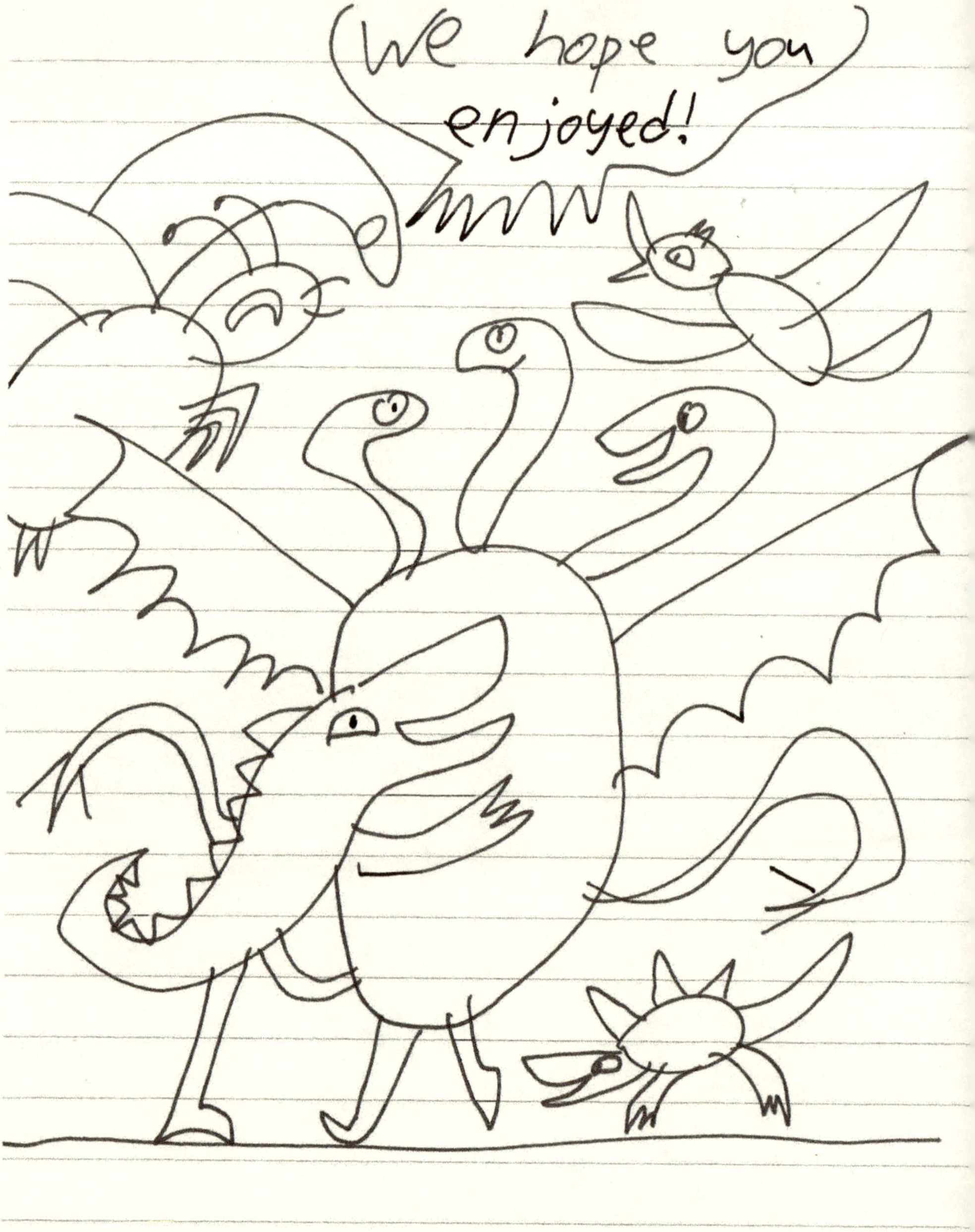
(We hope you enjoyed!)

Next the kaiju

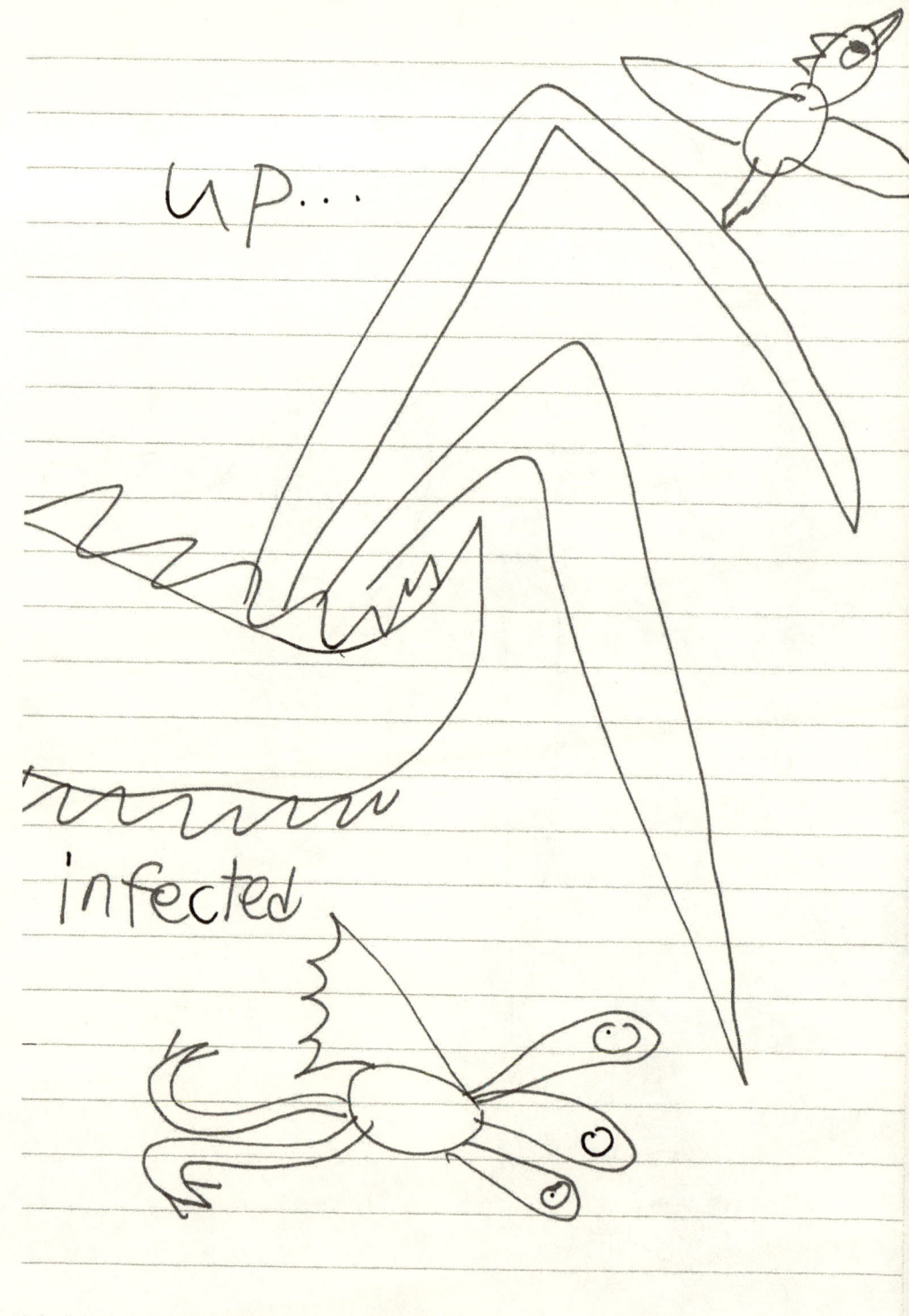

www.ingramcontent.com/pod-product-compliance
Lightning Source LLC
Chambersburg PA
CBHW032116090426
42743CB00007B/369